AF448120

POETIC WISDOM FOR LIFE

Proverbs 3:5-6

NANCY WERNER

Published by Innovo Publishing, LLC
www.innovopublishing.com
1-888-546-2111

Innovo Publishing LLC is a Christ-centered publisher located near Memphis, TN. Since 2008, Innovo has published quality books, eBooks, audiobooks, music, screenplays, and online and physical curricula that support the Great Commission, equip believers, and help create a positive Christian worldview. Innovo's capabilities and global reach provide Christian authors, artists, and ministries access to the world for Christ. To learn more about Innovo Publishing, visit our website at innovopublishing.com. To connect with other Christian creatives and to learn best practices for creating, publishing, marketing, and selling Christian titles, visit the Christian Publishing Portal at cpportal.com.

ROCKS ON THE PATH
Poetic Wisdom for Life

ISBN: 979-8-88928-074-3

Cover Design & Interior Layout: Innovo Publishing, LLC

Printed in the United States of America
U.S. Printing History
First Edition: 2025

Contents

Author's Note

I don't remember exactly how old I was when I started writing poetry. I know I was just a kid, and my family always encouraged me in the endeavor. However, the inspiration behind the poems was always God.

We lived on a farm, and everything around me was created by God—from the sweet hay fields and blackjack oaks to the cattle and corn and the butterflies and ants, God's hand was there in everything. Ours was a godly home, and God was the center of everything, and that included my creative ambitions. It is by God's inspiration that I was able to write these poems, and it is for God's glory that I penned them in this book.

Life can be a struggle sometimes, and if you are a Jesus follower, you will certainly have trials. My poems speak to those trials and the God who walks with us through them, guiding our steps on the path of life. May these poems be a light to you when you come across rocks on your path.

God
the Great Creator

I know my God, that He is real,
Although the world denies.
I know He's real and on the cross
He gave His Son to die.
He lives within this heart of mine
And His Holy Spirit guides me.
I live each day knowing that
My Savior walks beside me.
Though some deny and call Him false
Faithful to Him I'll be,
For He is the true and only God
The great Creator is He.

Nancy Werner

Reflections . . .

God
Is Real

I hear some say there is no God, and that they
don't believe.
They think somehow this world appeared without
Your mighty deeds.
But how could one imagine that the soaring
of a hawk
Or the radiance of a sunset took so little thought?
That it all should just appear without a
hand Divine,
To place them in the sky and make them
so sublime?
How could one see the ocean and the waves
so great and strong,
And not think a Creator sat upon the throne?

I look upon creation, from the ant to the sky,
And see such intricate beauty that God I
cannot deny.
The delicacy of an orchid, the mockingbird's
sweet song,
The majesty of the mountains, by omnipotence
were honed.
Though some may not believe in the existence of
my Lord,
I know without a doubt He created all this world.
In the fragrance of a rose or the rough bark
of the oak,
I know with all my heart, it came to be when my
Father spoke.
So doubt God if you will and say you don't believe,
But one day you will realize that you have
been deceived.
For all will stand before Him on the day he
has decreed,
And all will bow and know the truth . . . and
then you will believe.

Reflections . . .

Nancy Werner

He
Is Risen

"He is not here, He is risen,"
Is what the angel said.
"Why are you seeking
The living among the dead?
The Christ you saw crucified
And dying on the tree
Has risen from the grave
And offers life to those who believe."

On the cross He shed His lifeblood,
An atonement for the lost.
Risen, He is victorious,
The King of Kings, who bore our cross.

Nancy Werner

Reflections . . .

God
Is Sovereign

Do you live as God requires?
Do you walk with Him each day?
Do you surround yourselves with others
Who walk in Jesus' way?
Do you recognize God's sovereignty,
Or do you make Him small
So you can overlook Him
And not honor Him at all?
God is truly sovereign.
This world is in His hands.
He possesses all knowledge,
This you need to understand.
He knows the heart of every man,
Every woman, every child.
There is nothing hidden
From our Savior meek and mild.
But do not think this Savior
Will overlook your sin.
He also is your Judge and King;
You will answer to Him.
Fear the Lord and become wise,
Or else you will fall.
God is sovereign above all else.
God is sovereign over all.

Nancy Werner

Reflections . . .

Unconditional *Love*

Why did He love me,
Wretched soul that I am?
Worthy of nothing,
Especially not Him.
Yet still He came
And He chose to die
To save a sinner
As worthless as I.
Love so unselfish
Given for me,
To die such a death
On a cross, on a tree.
I'll never know why
He would choose to love me,
But because of this love
I now can live free.
Love so unconditional
I can't comprehend,
That He'd choose to die
That I might live through Him.

Nancy Werner

Reflections . . .

What
Love

I'm small and insignificant,
And yet I am loved
By God, the Holy Father,
And Jesus Christ, His Son.
I know that I'm worth nothing,
Yet Jesus came to die,
Sent by God, the Father,
A substitute for I.
He took my sin, bore my shame,
He left His throne on High
To carry my cross, shed His blood,
And in my place to die.
What love, what grace, what mercy
Was poured out on me
By the shed blood of Jesus
When He died upon the tree.
I owe my life to Jesus,
Who bore the cross for me,
And I will always serve Him
Who died and rose for me.

Nancy Werner

Reflections . . .

God Is Faithful
When We Are Not

God is faithful when we are not,
And yet He loves us still.
So much so He sent His Son
To die on Calvary's hill.
A love so great we don't deserve,
Yet still He gave His Son
So that we could be redeemed
By this precious Holy One.
The God-man, who knew no sin,
Took our place and died
So that we might have new life
And in His will abide.
If we accept His precious gift,
His mercy and His grace,
Then we should walk and bear the cross
Of the One who took our place.
Eternal life He offers us
And a home for eternity,
If we will just accept Him
And confess upon our knees.
No greater love has anyone
Than for a friend to die.
Jesus showed the greatest love
When He died for you and I.

Nancy Werner

Reflections . . .

Greater
Love

He walked hemmed in by soldiers,
His heart was filled with grief,
His flesh was raw and bloody,
His breath was slow and weak.
Wounds deep and ragged
from thorns thrust on His head,
His beard plucked in scorn
left His face swollen and red.
Despite these wounds so savage
and the torture that He bore,
The sins He carried for mortal man
hurt Him even more.
Though He was the Son of God,
He chose this path to walk,
For there was no other way
to save a world so lost.
He left His home in heaven
to become our sacrifice,
The Lamb of God was crucified
to give eternal life.
He let them nail Him to the cross,
He didn't have to stay.
He could have called the angels
or simply walked away.

He allowed them to condemn Him,
He didn't say a word,
Fulfilling prophecy,
His voice would yet be heard.
And so He let them take Him
and scourge Him brutally.
They stripped Him, they mocked Him,
they beat Him savagely.
He let them crucify Him
and hang Him on the tree,
Where He suffered intense pain
and brutal agony.
What great love our Lord must have,
such cruelty to go through,
To be the final sacrifice,
redeeming me and you.
In a borrowed tomb they laid Him
and put the stone in place,
But He rose again, He conquered death,
for all the human race.
The grave could not hold Him,
death could not win.
Jesus has the victory,
and life belongs to Him.
Greater love has no one
than to die for his friends,
And that is what Jesus calls
those who live for Him.

Reflections . . .

Nancy Werner

A Light
in the Darkness

A light in the darkness
God calls us to be
That others might find
The God that they need.
If we walk in the darkness,
We can't be that light,
And others will falter
In the black of the night.
If we walk with God
As He called us to do,
Our light will guide others
To the light of His truth.
Let your light shine
That all men may see
And glorify God
Who gave it to thee.

Nancy Werner

Reflections . . .

Am I
Hungry or Satisfied?

Am I hungry or satisfied?
Do I seek God's will or feel gratified?
Am I content to sit and wait,
Not seeking Him, not sharing His fate?
Do I truly know Christ, my Lord,
When I do not read His Holy Word?
When His commands I fail to keep,
Content to be a dismal sheep?
Satisfied to sit and wait,
While others work and grow in faith?
No, not for me.
To be satisfied,
I hunger and thirst to know God on high.
To the work and to the Word
That I might know better my blessed Lord,
Then satisfied I will one day be
When He calls me home to eternity.

Nancy Werner

Reflections . . .

When the
Way Gets Rough

Times are trying, this I know,
But God did say it would be so.
And even though the way gets rough,
It is in God we put our trust.
Though smooth the way may not be,
With rocks on the path and storms at sea,
God will never leave us there
Without Him being there to share
All the troubles and trials of life,
All the tears and all the strife.
When tired and weary from life's pitfalls,
The Lord will see us through them all.
God can turn the worst despair
Into faith and hope through our prayers.
All things work for good, said He,
If Him you love and Him you seek.
No matter what each day may bring,
God is sovereign over all things.
So put your faith in Him alone,
And God will see you safely home.
Put your trust alone in God
Who guides us on the path we trod.

Nancy Werner

Reflections . . .

Will You
Live for God?

Where does God fit in your life
Or have you room for Him?
Is everything else more important
Than living your life for Him?
He has given you life and breath;
Every second, minute, and hour,
And everything that you possess
He's allowed you to acquire.
Have you given Him the time of day
Or gotten on your knees to pray?
Did you thank Him for your very life
That He might require of you tonight?

Jesus gave His very life,
He is the ultimate sacrifice,
That you might live your life for Him
Forgiven of each and every sin.
"Be you holy as I am holy,"
The Lord God has said.
Live a life of righteousness
As Jesus, our example, did.
By grace He has saved you
If in Him you put your trust,
But God has also called you
To a life in His service.
What you sow, you will also reap
So this you must decide:
Will you live each day for Him
Or in your sin abide?

Reflections . . .

Nancy Werner

Lord,
That I Might Be

Oh dear Lord, that I might be
Closer every day to Thee.
Guide me by Thy Spirit true
That I might live pleasing to You.
Show me the path You'd have me take
And help me not Thy laws to break.
Make me a vessel Thy will to do
To work for Thee faithful and true.
Your grace has saved my soul from death
To live a life of righteousness!
May I ever Your servant be
To love and work and live for Thee.

Nancy Werner

Reflections . . .

Holiness

Do we strive to live in holiness
As we live from day to day?
Do we take the time each morning
To get on our knees and pray?
Do we take life for granted
And live any way we please
And disregard His Holy Word
For a life of sin and ease?
He will not overlook our sin
That so easily we commit,
For He has instructed us to
Live a life of holiness.
"Be ye Holy for I am Holy,"
Our God has commanded us.
Submit yourselves therefore to God
And flee all sinful lusts.
For we will not go guiltless
Or escape His punishment
If we continue to live in sin
And reject His holiness.

Nancy Werner

Reflections . . .

Pleasing
God

This life is so uncertain
And there are no guarantees
What we will face tomorrow,
So we best be on our knees,
Praying to the Father,
Who knows what is to come,
And ask Him for His guidance
As well as His wisdom.
Our God will never fail us
Though others round us do;
Our God will never leave us
But will always see us through.
God loves us, that is certain,
Although I'm not sure why,
I fail and falter daily,
But still He's by my side.
I love Him and I'll serve Him
The very best I can.
I'll follow where He leads me,
I'll hold His nail-scarred hand.
I want to please my Father
And grow in faith and love,
So I'll dig deep in His scripture
And cling to His great love.

Nancy Werner

Reflections . . .

Devoted to You

This world cannot stand,
I know this is true.
As time grows short
I'm devoted to You.
You shed Your lifeblood
And died on a tree
To save a sinner,
A wretch like me.
Devoted to You
With heart and soul,
You are my Lord,
And You're in control.
May all that I do
Glorify Your name.
Devoted to You,
I am not ashamed.
You are my Savior,
You are my Lord.
Devoted to You,
I live by Your Word.
My life is Yours,
I'm gladly Your slave,
Devoted to You
All of my days!

Nancy Werner

Reflections . . .

Forgiven

Looking back over the years of my life,
I see many struggles, I see much strife.
I see where I depended on myself alone,
And lost my way and did much wrong.
Too many times I went my own way
And found there were consequences to pay.
I promised I'd walk with God long ago,
But let the winds of life toss me to and fro.
The desires of the world seemed to overcome
And they left me empty, tired, and ruined.
Darkness dwells where God is not,
And I walked in darkness an awful lot!
In the light of day, in the sun's bright light,
I felt the darkness grip me tight.
Even when the sun shines bright,
If God's not there, there is no light.
Mistakes I've made, hard lessons learned,
But still God loves this little worm.
I know I've caused Him loads of grief
And caused Him often to mourn and weep.
Still, He forgave my every sin
And let me start anew again.
Greater Love has never been
Than He who died to save from sin!

Nancy Werner

Reflections . . .

Serving *Him*

I dreamed I stood at heaven's gate
And fear gripped my heart.
The Savior had died to save me,
But I had not done my part.
I believed in His love and forgiveness,
But my life did not change by much.
I lived mostly as I always had
But believed that that was enough.
Now standing before the gates of heaven,
I hung my head in shame.
My Savior had sacrificed His life
And I'd done nothing for His name.
He gave His all, but I gave nothing,
No light in the darkness was I.
A stumbling block to others? Yes!
This I could not deny.
His commandments I failed to keep;
His Word I rarely opened;

I didn't even love enough
To try to get to know Him.
I knew the Words that I would hear
When I finally stood before Him,
"Depart from me," the Lord would say,
Because I never knew Him.
Bitter tears stained my cheeks
As I fell before heaven's gates.
Too late now to repent and cry.
Hell would be my fate.
I awakened then in the cold dark night.
The dream still clear before me.
I fell to my knees in bitter tears
And asked God to forgive me.
My life is His, I live for Him;
His commandments are sweet to me.
His Word I treasure in my heart
And I'm daily on my knees.
Life did not get easier
Because I trusted Him,
But serving Him has made my life
What it always should have been.

Reflections . . .

Nancy Werner

Forsaken

We have lost our way. It is sad but true.
We don't celebrate Christmas as we used to do.
Once we celebrated the birth of Christ,
Now it's an offense to speak of His life.
The Creator of all, the King of kings,
This world has dubbed as not worth a thing.
May God forgive us for what we have done
In dishonoring Him and His only true Son.
I pray that all everywhere would repent.
Maybe, if we do, then God will relent,
For this world is on the brink of despair,
Spiraling downward with never a care.
His judgement is just. We are to blame.
We've forsaken our God and dishonored His name.

Nancy Werner

Reflections . . .

How Oft
I Fail

Lord, how oft I fail You
And hang my head in shame.
My intentions may be well meant,
But I fail You just the same.
My good intentions all fall flat,
For I take my eyes off You.
In doing so I forget Your Word
And do things I should not do.
Then those things bring me sorrow,
Sin, ruin, and despair.
Then misery descends on me
For I'm caught in Satan's snares.
In my distress, I call to You,
And You hear my feeble cry.
And in Your grace and mercy
You forgive such as I.
By this I know You love me,
For You convict me of my sin,
And when I come in repentance,
I receive Your love again.
My prayer is to be faithful,
Devoted to Your Word,
Obedient to Your commandments,
To grow more like You, my Lord.

Nancy Werner

Reflections . . .

The
Healer

No one sees the inside
Shattered by life and sin.
They only glimpse the outside
While the turmoil hides within.
But God, the great Healer,
Mends the shattered soul
And brings the brokenhearted
Back into the fold.
He picked up all the pieces
That lie shattered in a pile
And put me back together
With love and time and a smile.
Scars, yes, I have some,
But Jesus has some too.
I'm finally back "together,"
But I struggle sometimes too.
It hasn't been an easy road,
Sometimes it isn't still.
At first it was a mountain,
But now it's just a hill.
I've learned that life's not easy,
It can tear your world apart,
But God can fix the shattered life
And mend the broken heart!

Nancy Werner

Reflections . . .

Never
Forsaken

When I need peace and quiet
And the world is closing in,
I run to God in prayer
And confess my every sin.
Then I ask Him for His comfort
To see me through the day,
For I know without Him
I will not find my way.
When I am lost or lonely
And all have left my side,
I know that He is with me
And He will be my guide.
He never has forsaken me
And I know He never will.
When the storms of life assail me
His hand, the wind will still.
I know no matter where I go
That He will be beside me,
A constant Friend and Father
Who will always help and guide me.
His love is unconditional
And is offered to us all
Through the blood of Christ, His Son,
He has offered life to all.

Nancy Werner

Reflections . . .

Reflections . . .

When
I Am Weak

When I am weak, what do I do?
I get on my knees, and I cry to You.
I ask for Your help, I ask for Your strength,
I ask for Your patience, I ask for Your peace.
When I am weak and I call to You,
You answer my cry and help me get through.
You give me the strength I need to go on.
Through troubles and trials, You give me a song.
My Father, my God, my Friend ever true.
As long as I trust You, You will see me through.

Nancy Werner

Reflections . . .

When
I Fell

I remember when I fell away,
It haunts me to this very day.
I allowed someone to take God's place
And control my life and turn my face.
I ignored God's warnings, to please another,
And life became a constant struggle.
I lost my family, I lost my way,
I lost my God, forgot the price He paid.
I let that person take control
And almost lost my very soul.
Finally life came crashing down,
And I found the courage to turn around.
I left that person far behind
And in doing so found peace of mind.
Regained my family, reclaimed my life,
Restored the best relationship of my life.
To God, my Father, I did return,
But a hard lesson I had to learn.
God must be first in each one's life
Or else all is vain and misery and strife.

Nancy Werner

Reflections . . .

The Mountain
I Must Climb

Lord, as I face this mountain
That stands before me here,
I wonder how I'll climb it,
I wonder if You are near.
It looks so steep and jagged
And makes me feel so small.
I'm afraid that it will crush me.
I'm afraid that I will fall.

"My child, do not be fearful
As you climb this mountain high,
For I'll be climbing with you,
I'll be right by your side.
Do not fear the mountain
Or the jagged path you see,
For it will not defeat you,
Just keep your eyes on Me."

"Together we will climb it,
Together we'll laugh and cry.
We'll share all the good times
And put the bad behind.
I am your Faithful Father,
I loved you before time began.
I will never let you fall,
You are safe in the palm of My hand."

Nancy Werner

Reflections . . .

Aging

Dear Lord, please hear my humble prayer
and help me every day
To walk, to work, to just survive
as my life and body age.
I cannot do what once I could,
and Lord, it's hard to take.
Once I worked the hours through
never needing to take a break.
But now the breaks are often,
and the pain grows every day.
Muscles that once were strong
seem to have faded fast away.
I ask You, Lord, to help me
and maybe give relief
To the tired and aching muscles
that now cause so much grief.
I know that this is normal,
our bodies weren't meant to last,
But it doesn't make it easier
knowing all of that.

Time has taken its toll on me,
and that I must confess,
But truly I wish with all my heart
that the pain could please be less.
I try to do the best I can,
but it doesn't seem enough
Compared to the days gone by
when I could do so much.
It's hard to accept, Lord,
that I never will again
Be the strong and viral youth
that I was way back then.
So now I think of heaven
and the new body I'll receive
And, Lord, I will be thankful
this old one here to leave.
But, Lord, til that day happens,
I ask you please for strength
To endure the pain I must,
but also request relief.
Relief, if You will, Lord,
from the pain that never leaves
So that what life here remains
may be enjoyed with a little ease.

Reflections . . .

Nancy Werner

Eternity

Do you know where you'll spend eternity?
Have you given it any thought?
Will you walk through the gates of heaven,
Or will hell be the place you sought?
There's more to being a Christian
Than walking down the aisle,
And don't think you'll get in heaven
Because you were baptized back a while.
You can go to church on Sunday,
But it's not going to get you in.
Either you've been pardoned by God
Or you'll be punished for your sin.

If your life does not mirror
The Christ who died for you,
You'd better start rethinking
What you've chosen to say and do!
If you never read your Bible,
If you never take time to pray,
If you don't live the Ten Commandments,
You might just be turned away.
God's Word says He is a jealous God;
He demands obedience from His own.
Don't think you can live any way you want
And still call heaven your home.
Do you know where you'll spend eternity?
Have you given it any thought?
Will you walk through the gates of heaven,
Or will hell be the place you sought?

Reflections . . .

Nancy Werner

Heaven
or Hell?

There is a choice we each must make
As to our destiny.
We can choose the God of heaven
Or hell for eternity.
We can live for Him or die in sin,
The choice is ours to make.
God won't make you walk with Him;
We each must choose our fate.
He sent His Son, His precious Son,
To die for you and me,
To take our sins upon Himself
That we might all live free.
You will find forgiveness
If you choose Jesus Christ,
Or reject Him completely
And lose eternal life.
The choice is yours. You must decide
If you love your sin so well
That you reject the Christ who died.
Will you choose heaven or hell?

Nancy Werner

Reflections . . .

The Fool
Has Said

The fool has said there is no God
And lives in sin and lust.
He takes his pleasures at his will
Til he returns to dust.
Then judgment comes upon him
And his heart is filled with dread
As he stands before the God
That he assumed was dead.
No salvation for the fool,
Only eternal death.
He faces condemnation,
No joy, no peace, no rest.
Here he mocked God's children
And denied God's holy name.
His life was corrupt and evil
And the righteous he did disdain.
Be not as the foolish man
Who rejects the Father and Son,
Whose end will end in torment
For the deeds that he has done.
Seek the Christ who died for you
And choose to live for Him,
For no other name under heaven
Can save us from our sin.

Nancy Werner

Reflections . . .

The Man
on the Third Cross

The Man on the third cross,
Pure and innocent was He.
He took my place and died,
He bore my penalty.
Love beyond all measure
Displayed in that One's death
To take my filthy sins
Upon His precious breast.
Oh, how I don't deserve it,
The shame He bore for me,
The stripes upon His sinless back,
The horrible agony.
Oh, how some despise Him,
This Jesus called the Christ,
But this act of love was offered
To save this sinner's life.
Despise Him not, oh sinner.
Get down upon your knees,
Repent to your Creator
Who died to set you free.

Nancy Werner

Reflections . . .

Too Much
of the World

Is there too much of the world in you
To distract you from your Lord?
Would you rather read a novel
Than delve into His Word?
Would you rather play a game,
Watch a movie, catch a show,
Than spend some time with Jesus
And Him to get to know?
Is football more important
Than the worship of the Lord?
Is Sunday just another day,
Not a Sabbath to the Lord?
Are you too busy "living"
To think about your life?
How little time you give Him,
Who gave for you His life!

What direction are you heading
That you have no time for Him?
You'd rather do "your own thing."
Don't you know that that's a sin?
And when you stand before Him
On the Judgment Day,
What will you say to Him
When you see Him face to face?
You may say you know Him
Then be left in utter despair,
When Jesus turns you away
For you had not the time to care!
To love Him is to serve Him.
It is not a life of ease.
It is a life of sacrifice,
Unselfish, Him to please.
If the world is more important
Than what you do for Him,
You're going down the wrong road,
Headed for a bitter end!

Reflections . . .

Nancy Werner

Choose
This Day

The world is growing darker,
Evil is being called good.
Even those called Christians
Aren't living as they should.
They preach an easy gospel,
They all say God is love,
They say that all is relative
So bad is really good.
God is love, I know that's true,
But God is so much more.
He calls Himself a jealous God,
He won't tolerate this world.
Our God abhors evil
And hates our every sin.
You can't live like Satan
And hope to "enter in."

The gate is straight and narrow
That leads to heaven's shore.
The broad gate won't get you there,
No, it leads to hell's front door.
Wake up, my friend, and understand
Your tolerance of sin is wrong
And it won't get you anywhere
If you're singing the wrong song.
God's wrath will fall on sinners
Who refuse to repent of sin
And on "so-called" Christians
Who live as sinful men.
If you don't stand for Jesus
As His Word commands us to,
You better just get ready
Cause His wrath will fall on you.
God is sovereign over all.
We all are His creation.
Choose this day who you will serve,
The God of heaven, or hell and Satan.

Reflections . . .

Nancy Werner

For God
So Loved

Jesus prayed in the garden,
"Let this cup pass from me."
His sweat dropped as blood
In Gethsemane.
Great sorrow He felt
As He knelt and prayed,
Knowing exactly
Where His destiny lay.
He had to die
So that we might live,
For only His blood
Would cleanse us from sin.
He bore the cross,
He bore the shame,
We can only gain life
Through His precious name.
For God so loved,
His Son He gave,
And only through Him
Can we be saved.

Nancy Werner

Reflections . . .

Free
Gift

Oh Lord, I know there is nothing
that I could ever do
While living on this earth
to earn eternal life with You.
I am a wretched sinner
who was bound for hell and lost,
But You gave Your life for me,
You paid the awful cost.
Because You made the sacrifice
and shed Your precious blood,
I can have eternal life
and share in Your great love.
Repentant at Your feet I bowed
and gave to You my life,
To live and love and serve Thee
through joy or through strife.
I could never earn Your love
or work enough for Thee,
For I am only human,
but Your gift of life is free!

By grace I'm saved and not my works,
for they would never do
To earn me a place in heaven—no,
I must trust in You.
You became the sacrifice
because I never could
Live up to what it takes to earn
a place in heaven above.
Because of what You did in love,
I will serve You all my days,
I'll strive to live in holiness
and walk in all Your ways.
Though I falter daily
and fall short at every turn,
I know Your grace has saved me,
it is nothing I can earn.
Thank You for such precious love
to become my sacrifice
And take my place on Calvary
to save my worthless life.
I can never do enough
to show my gratitude,
But I will live my entire life
surrendered, Lord, to You.

Reflections . . .

Nancy Werner

The Cross Was Not Pretty

The cross was not pretty
Like the trinkets we wear.
It was bloody, it was brutal,
The cross Christ did bear.
But what held Him there
On that torturous tree?
It was not the nails,
No . . . it was me!
He was mocked and beaten.
He was tortured; scourged.
He carried upon Him
My sins and yours.
The cross, it was heavy.

His flesh, ripped and torn,
His body racked with pain.
Yet for this He was born.
What kind of love
This love must be
That He chose to die
For someone like me!
He drank from the cup,
So bitter and cruel,
Choosing to die
For a lost fallen world.
When I think of the pain
And the sheer agony
That He chose to bear
That I might live free,
My heart filled with shame
I confess all my sin,
And He forgives me
Because I accept Him.

Reflections . . .

Nancy Werner

Sin's
Dark Night

There is a darkness
That pulls at me,
Trying to drown me
In a deep black sea.
It hovers over me
Like a deep black veil.
It's blackness scares me
And speaks of hell.
It's the darkness of sin
From a guilty heart
That craves salvation
Only God can impart.

To hold on to sin,
Like a dear old friend,
Without repentance
Brings a bitter end.
Repentance only
To the God of heaven
Is the only way
To be forgiven.
And with forgiveness
Comes the Light,
Freed from the darkness
Of sin's dark night.
The Light of redemption
Is our Lord Jesus Christ,
Our Savior who died
To pay the ultimate price.

Reflections . . .

Nancy Werner

A Prayer

Oh Lord, I pray for mercy,
Of which we don't deserve.
The world is growing darker
And does not heed Your Word.
I pray blind eyes would open
And see the Truth You are,
That hearts would turn and seek You
Before they've gone too far;
Too far in sin and evil
And the lusts of their hearts,
And they be lost forever
In hell's torment, oh so dark.
I pray for Your children
Who stand faithful and true.
Though hated, persecuted,
Just because we love You.
Give us strength whatever comes,
And help us to endure,
And guide us through the turmoil here
To walk on heaven's shores.

Nancy Werner

Reflections . . .

Selfish Lives

People live such selfish lives
With no regard for God.
They do not take the time to pray
Before their morning starts.
They rush around, too busy
To read His Word or pray.
They take their God for granted
Every single day.
They forget God is Creator,
They forget GOD IS GOD,
He is the sovereign Great I Am,
Enthroned in heaven above.

They really do not fear Him,
It seems they do not know
That it doesn't matter what they do,
God is in control.
He is Lord and Master,
The universe is His.
Only He can save us,
But we must turn to Him.
Continue to walk contrary
To the will of God,
Putting worldly life before Him
Is a dangerous path to trod.
For when you stand before Him
On the Judgment Day,
If you did not live for Him,
You will be turned away.

Reflections . . .

Nancy Werner

Prayer
for Troubled Times

Oh Lord, this world is troubled,
But You are in control.
And though it seems so hopeless
You will not let us go.
You cover us with Your wings
And we find shelter there.
And though the world is reeling,
We still find safety there.
You said You would not leave us
Comfortless while here,
And though sometimes it's hard
I know You're always near.
You are there beside us
Whatever comes our way,
And You will see us through
Each and every day.
So, Lord, when I get worried,
When all this world seems wrong,
Help me to remember
That You're still on Your Throne.

Nancy Werner

Reflections . . .

Joy
Inexpressible

I know this world is growing dark,
But I won't let the darkness in
Because I know that You are God
And my real home is heaven.
Sometimes I get discouraged
When I listen to the news,
But You are greater than all the deeds
That the evil doers do.
My faith is still in You, Lord,
And not in this old world.
The world may rant and riot,
But sovereignty is Yours.
It's easy to get down and cry
And feel it's just no use,

But You told us this would come to pass,
We've heard it from our youth.
This world will grow dark and evil,
And men will turn away.
We will have tribulation,
We are seeing it every day.
You told us this would happen,
But the world You've overcome,
So we may still have hope
Even though the darkness looms.
Our hope is not in this world
But in the world to come
Where You will reign forever
And we truly will be home.
Let us, as Your Word proclaims,
While among the human race,
Rejoice with joy inexpressible,
The outcome of our faith.

Reflections . . .

Nancy Werner

End Times
Prayer

Sometimes we get discouraged, Lord,
Sometimes angry, sometimes sad,
Because the world we're living in
Is getting to be so bad.
We read Your Word and understand
That evil does exist;
That Satan lives and breathes
And shakes his ugly fist.
We know the end is nearing, Lord,
The time is now at hand
For prophecies to be fulfilled
All across the land.
I pray that we can turn the tide
Of evil in our land,
But when I see the world events
I know we cannot stand
Unless we turn, our sins confess,
And forsake our evil ways.
For there is no other course
For this judgment to be stayed.

Nancy Werner

Reflections . . .